PLAY PUCCINI
VIOLIN

10 Arias Transcribed for Intermediate Violin & Piano

Transcribed & Edited by Paolo Toscano

To access companion recorded performances and accompaniments online, visit:
www.halleonard.com/mylibrary

Enter Code
1079-2611-7829-7780

ISBN 978-0-634-04634-6

RICORDI

DISTRIBUTED BY

7777 W. BLUEMOUND RD. P.O. BOX 13819 MILWAUKEE, WI 53213

www.halleonard.com
www.ricordi.com

The operas of Italian composer **Giacomo Puccini** (1858-1924) are among the most popular in the world. With their soaring melodies and expressive harmonies, they are the most directly emotional pieces ever written for the lyric theater.

Puccini was born into a musical family, one that had provided his hometown of Lucca, Italy with church organists and composers for four generations. Puccini learned the basics of music from one of his uncles; his father died when Puccini was only five years old. As a boy, Giacomo sang in the local church choirs, and by age 14 was substituting for the organists.

The cultural life in Lucca was unusually active for such a provincial town. The plays and operas Puccini saw there in his formative years had a profound effect on him. His early exposure to many different kinds of theatrical productions helped develop his ability to discover the operatic possibilites of plays which he saw as an adult, such as *Tosca* and *Madam Butterfly*.

Giacomo entered the Milan Conservatory at the late age of 22. His composition teachers were Antonio Bazzini and, later, Amilcare Ponchielli, who wrote the famous opera *La Gioconda* ("The Joyful Girl"). His experiences during the three years he spent as a poor student in Milan have much in common with the starving artists he later depicted in his most popular opera, *La bohème* ("The Bohemian Life").

While a student at the conservatory, Puccini entered a competition for one-act operas. Though his opera *Le villi* did not win, it brought him to the attention of music publisher Giulio Ricordi, who commissioned a second opera from Puccini (*Edgar*), instituting a lifelong association between the composer and the publishing house Casa Ricordi. Signor Giulio became a father figure for Puccini, acting as his advisor and agent, and publishing eleven operas.

Puccini's life had its share of scandal. About the time he was working on *Edgar*, Puccini began an affair with Elvira Gemignani, the wife of a Luccan merchant, who bore him a son in 1886. Elvira's union with Puccini was not legalized until 1904, after the death of her husband. Later, after a servant girl committed suicide, Puccini and his wife were at the center of a press frenzy, causing everyone to remark on how like a tragic opera the composer's life had become.

Entirely a man of the theater, Puccini composed only a few pieces aside from his operas. He once wrote: "Almighty God touched me with His little finger and said 'Write for the theater—mind, only for the theater.' And I have obeyed the supreme command." For him, theater possessed ideals that were resolute and changeless: he believed theater must interest, surprise, touch, or provoke laughter. Puccini constantly lived up to this credo in his operas.

Puccini's approach to composition was theatrically driven. He worked closely with his librettists to shape the operas in a way which made dramatic sense. The composer gave each opera its own unique orchestral color, and highlighted particularly dramatic moments by using harmonies which were modern and forward-looking for their time. He allowed the strong emotions of the characters to come to the fore through their appealing, straightforward vocal melodies.

Instrumentalists are often encouraged to imitate a singer's phrasing and expressive fluidity of tone. Though these *Play Puccini* arrangements are not technically difficult, there is an inherent challenge in their *musical* elements. Players should not be self-conscious about infusing their performances with more emotion than usual, using the opera plot notes as a point of departure.

CONTENTS

The price of this publication includes access to companion recorded performances and accompaniments online, for download or streaming, using the unique code found on the title page.
Visit **www.halleonard.com/mylibrary** and enter the access code.

4

LA BOHÈME [lah boh-**ehm**] (The Bohemian Life)
Opera in 4 acts
Libretto by Giuseppe Giacosa and Luigi Illica, after Henry Murger's novel *Scènes de la vie de bohème*
First performance: Teatro Regio, Turin, 1 February 1896

The story of this opera, one of the best loved in the repertory, is set in 1830s Paris, though productions of the opera are often set in the 1890s, the period of the opera's composition. Four friends share a garret apartment: the poet Rodolfo, the painter Marcello, the musician Schaunard, and the philosopher Colline. On a cold Christmas Eve, Rudolfo sends his roommates out to the Cafè Momus while he tries to finish writing a newspaper article. His neighbor Mimi, a seamstress, knocks on the door and asks him to light her candle. The two are immediately attracted to each other, and when Mimi "accidentally" drops her key and Rodolfo's candle "accidentally" goes out, they look for her key in the dark. They tell each other about themselves, and are singing a love duet by the end of the first act. In act two, they join the others at the Momus. Musetta, a coquettish cafè singer and Marcello's former lover, arrives, drawing attention to herself by singing the waltz-song "Quando men vo" [**kwan**-doh mehn voh] (When I go out). In the final act, Mimi is dying of tuberculosis and returns to the garret to be with Rodolfo. When left alone, Mimi and Rodolfo renew their love for each other and share reminiscences. With all their bohemian friends present, Mimi dies peacefully, as Rodolfo sobs over her lifeless body.

LA FANCIULLA DEL WEST [la-fahn-**choo**-lah dehl wehst] (The Girl of the Golden West)
Opera in 3 acts
Libretto by Carlo Zangarini and Guelfo Civinini, after David Belasco's play
First performance: Metropolian Opera, New York, 10 December 1910

This opera, commissioned by the Metropolitan opera, is set in a California mining camp during the 1849 gold rush. Minnie, proprietor of the Polka Saloon, is adored and respected by the miners. She falls in love with Dick Johnson, a newcomer. Johnson is really the hunted bandit Ramerrez, but he tells her he wants to change his ways because of his love for her. After he is shot by a posse, Minnie protects Johnson by hiding him in her house, but Sheriff Jack Rance finds him there. Minnie challenges the sheriff to a poker game over Johnson, which she wins by cheating. Johnson is allowed to escape briefly, but is soon caught and sentenced to die by hanging. With a noose around his neck, he sings the aria "Ch'ella mi creda" [**kehl**-lah mee **kray**-dah] (Let her believe), in which he asks the miners to let Minnie believe he has escaped. Minnie rides in and begs the miners, who dote on her, to allow the two of them to leave together. The miners agree, and Minnie and Dick ride off into the sunset, singing "Addio, California."

GIANNI SCHICCHI [**jahn**-nee **skee**-kee]
Opera in 1 act
Libretto by Giovacchino Forzano, suggested by an episode in Dante's *Inferno*
First performance: Metropolitan Opera, New York, 14 December 1918

This comic opera, the third part of *Il trittico* (The Triptych), relates the story of the crime for which Gianni Schicchi, a real-life character, is consigned to hell in Dante's *Divine Comedy*. The action is set in Florence, 1299. The recently-deceased Buoso Donati is surrounded by falsely grieving relatives who become outraged when they learn that his will leaves his entire estate to a monastery. Rinuccio, one of Donati's young nephews, is in love with Lauretta, but his family disapproves of this union because they believe she is not worthy of the family. It is Rinuccio who finds the will, but he refuses to hand it over until the family promises they will engage the cunning Gianni Schicchi, Lauretta's father, to help them out of their dilemma, and also consent to his wedding plans. When Schicchi arrives, he is loath to assist the money-hungry relatives. Lauretta, in love with Rinuccio, pleads with him in the famous aria "O mio babbino caro" [oh **mee**-oh bahb-**bee**-noh **kah**-roh] (O my beloved daddy). He agrees to help, orders the dead man removed, and warns the relatives of the punishment all will face if the plot is discovered (exile and the loss of a hand). He climbs into bed and dictates a new will to a gullible lawyer, leaving the choice items to himself and the house to Lauretta and Rinuccio.

MADAMA BUTTERFLY

Opera in 3 acts
Libretto by Giuseppe Giacosa and Luigi Illica, after the play by David Belasco,
      based on a story by John Luther Long
First performance: Teatro alla Scala, Milan, 17 February 1904

The opera takes place in Nagasaki, Japan in the early 1900s. Lieutenant Benjamin Franklin Pinkerton is an American naval officer stationed in Japan. Cio-Cio San, a 15-year-old geisha known as Madame Butterfly, has agreed to a broker-arranged marriage with him, giving up her religion for his and suffering the reproof of her family on her wedding day. Pinkerton is less serious about the union, toasting the day he will have a "real American wife." When he soon leaves for America, he promises to come back "when the robin nests." Cio-Cio San waits for him, now with his son whom she has borne. After three years with no word from him, Butterfly still believes he will return, singing "Un bel dì, vedremo" [oon behl dee veh-**dray**-moh] (One fine day, he will return). Despite a marriage proposal from a rich Japanese suitor and efforts from Sharpless to make the true situation known to her, Butterfly believes that if Pinkerton hears of his Japanese son, he will come back to her. Pinkerton's ship finally returns. Upon arriving at Butterfly's home while she is out, he realizes the cruelty of his actions. After he has left, Cio-Cio San rushes in expecting to find him there, but is faced with the truth in the person of the American wife, Kate Pinkerton. She will give up her son, she says, if Pinkerton will come for him in half an hour. Unwilling to live with such shame, Butterfly says goodbye to her child, stabs herself with her father's sword, and dies just as Pinkerton enters to claim the boy.

MANON LESCAUT [mah-nõ leh-**sko**]

Opera in 4 acts
Libretto by Marco Praga, Domenico Oliva, Giuseppe Giacosa, Luigi Illica,
      after Abbè Prèvost's novel *L'Histoire du Chevalier des Grieux et de Manon Lescaut*
First performance: Teatro Regio, Turin, 1 February 1893

The opera is set in France and Louisiana in the late eighteenth century. When the Chevalier des Grieux sees Manon for the first time, she is on her way to a convent, under the care of her brother. Des Grieux speaks to her, they fall immediately in love and run off to Paris, stealing a carriage in which wealthy old Geronte di Ravoir, the Treasurer General, had himself hoped to abduct the girl. Eventually Manon leaves des Grieux, unable to resist Geronte's money. Wishing she could be back in the humble setting where she was truly loved, she complains that in the silken curtains ("In quelle trine morbide") [een **kwel**-leh **tree**-neh **mohr**-bee-day] there is a chill that numbs her. When the Chevalier later reappears, the two pledge renewed love. Before fleeing together, Manon stops to gather up the jewels Geronte had lavished upon her. The delay is costly, for the police Geronte had summoned now enter and capture her. Manon is deported to Louisiana, and des Grieux insists on accompanying her. In New Orleans, des Grieux helps Manon escape, and they leave in search of an English settlement. At one point she finds herself ill, exhausted, and alone in the wilderness. When des Grieux returns, she dies in his arms.

SUOR ANGELICA [swor ahn-**geh**-lee-kah] (Sister Angelica)

Opera in 1 act
Libretto by Giovacchino Forzano
First performance: Metropolitan Opera, New York, 14 December 1918

This opera, the second part of *Il trittico* (The Triptych), is set in a convent near Siena in the seventeenth century. Sister Angelica, the daughter of a noble Florentine family, was forced to enter a convent after bearing a child out of wedlock seven years ago. Her aunt, the Princess, comes to ask her to sign away her inheritance. When Angelica asks for news about her child, she is told coldly that he has been dead for two years. She sings the heart-wrenching aria "Senza mamma" [**sehn**-zah **mahm**-mah] (Without a mother), then decides to commit suicide by drinking poison. In her dying moments, she prays for forgiveness and sees a vision of the Virgin Mary bringing her child to her.

TOSCA [**taw**-skah]

Opera in 3 acts
Libretto by Giuseppi Giacosa and Luigi Illica, after the play by Victorien Sardou
First performance: Teatro Costanzi, Rome, 14 January 1900

This popular melodrama is set in Rome, June 1800. The painter Mario Cavaradossi is in love with Floria Tosca, a famous singer. While working on a mural in the church of Sant'Andrea della Valle, he sings the aria "Recondita armonia" [ray-**kohn**-dee-tahr-moh-**nee**-ah] (Secret harmonies), comparing the portrait of Mary Magdalene he is painting to the dark-eyed Tosca. Tosca soon arrives at the church. When Angelotti, an escaped political prisoner, appears at the church, Cavaradossi offers to help him by hiding him at his house. Angelotti was imprisoned by Scarpia, the sadistic and hypocritical chief of police, for being active in the uprising to make Rome a republic. Scarpia, who is also in love with Tosca, has Cavaradossi arrested, interrogated, and finally tortured in order to learn where Angelotti is hiding. Tosca, who can hear her lover's tortured screams, pleads in vain with Scarpia to show mercy to Cavaradossi. Finally, to stop the torture, Tosca discloses Angelotti's hiding place. Scarpia signs the warrant for Cavaradossi's execution, but tells Tosca that if she will give herself to him, he will spare her lover's life. In a moment of despair she sings "Vissi d'arte" [**vee**-see **dahr**-tay] (I lived for art), a passionate outpouring of grief. When she agrees to Scarpia's bargain, he says a mock execution must be carried out, after which Tosca and Cavaradossi are free to make a getaway. As he turns to embrace her, Tosca stabs Scarpia with a knife from his supper table, killing him. Meanwhile, Cavaradossi is imprisoned in the Castel Sant'Angelo, awaiting death at dawn. He sings "E lucevan le stelle" [ay loo-**chay**-vahn lay **stehl**-lay] (And the stars were shining), a poignant aria in which he remembers Tosca and their love. Tosca arrives and tells him of Scarpia's death and the plan for the fake execution. When Cavaradossi fails to get up after the firing squad has left (Tosca believes the bullets are blanks), Tosca suddenly realizes her lover is dead; Scarpia has tricked her. Scarpia has been found murdered, and as the soldiers come for her, Tosca runs to the edge of the battlements and jumps off, killing herself.

TURANDOT [**too**-rahn-doht]

Opera in 3 acts
Libretto by Giuseppe Adami and Renato Simoni, after Friedrich von Schiller's adaptation
of the play *Turandotte* by Carlo Gozzi; also possibly after *The Arabian Nights*
First performance: Teatro alla Scala, Milan, 25 April 1926

The opera is set in Beijing in ancient times. The princess Turandot will marry the man who can solve three riddles; those who fail are summarily beheaded. Calaf, exiled prince of Tartary, is captured by her beauty and is willing to submit to the test, against the protests of his father, the exiled King Timur, and the faithful slave girl Liù, who is in love with him. Calaf wins the riddle contest, but Turandot still will not marry him. He, in turn, poses his own riddle for her: if she can tell him his name before daybreak, he will submit to execution. Turandot declares that no one shall sleep until the name of the prince is known, upon penalty of death. Calaf hears the injunction, but is unmoved: in "Nessun dorma" [**neh**-soon **dohr**-mah] (None shall sleep) he confidently states that he alone will unveil the secret, and when the sun is high in the heavens Turandot will indeed be his bride. Meanwhile, Timur and Liù are arrested and threatened with torture. Fearing for Timur's life, Liù says that she alone knows the name; she is tortured, but refuses to tell. When Turandot asks her what gives her such strength, she replies "Princess, it is love." In the emotional climax of the opera, Liù addresses Turandot directly, then stabs herself with a soldier's dagger. Alone with the icy princess after Liù's suicide, Calaf tears off Turandot's veil, gives her a passionate kiss, and provides her with the opportunity to execute him by revealing his name. She calls for her court to be assembled and proclaims to all the stranger's name: Love.

Quando men vo
(When I go out)

LA BOHÈME
(The Bohemian Life)

Giacomo Puccini

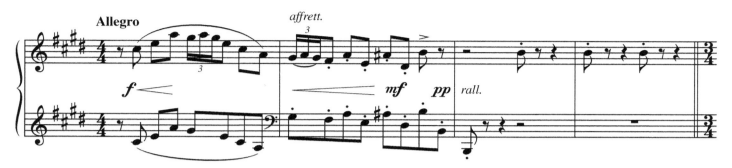

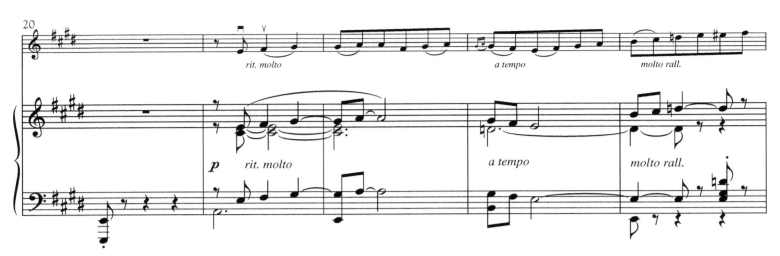

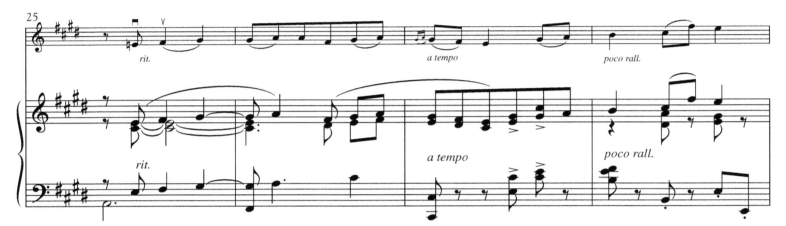

Ch'ella mi creda
(Let her believe)

LA FANCIULLA DEL WEST
(The Girl of the Golden West)

Giacomo Puccini

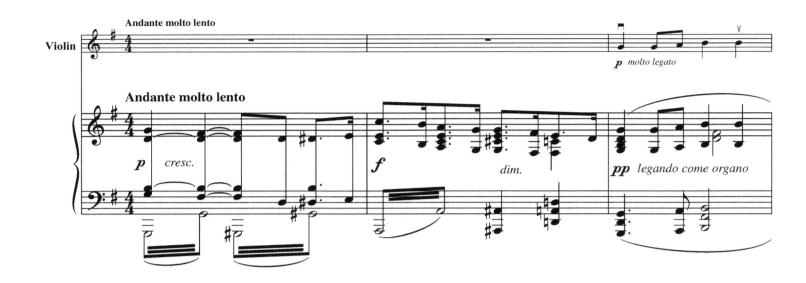

Un bel dì, vedremo
(One fine day, he will return)
MADAMA BUTTERFLY

Giacomo Puccini

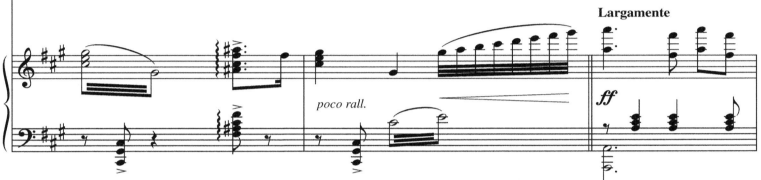

In quelle trine morbide

(In those soft curtains)

MANON LESCAUT

Giacomo Puccini

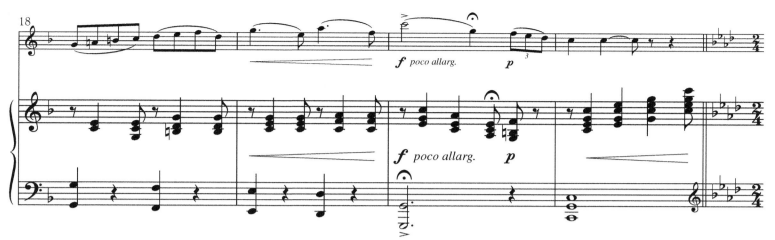

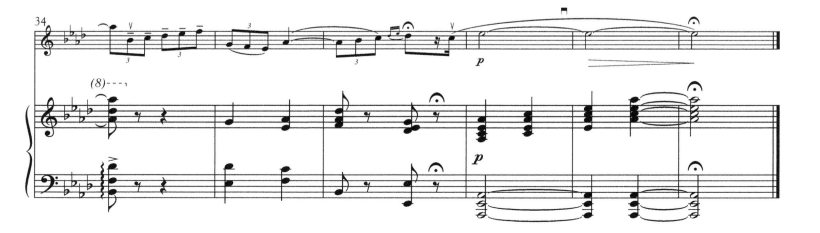

O mio babbino caro

(O my beloved daddy)

GIANNI SCHICCHI

Giacomo Puccini

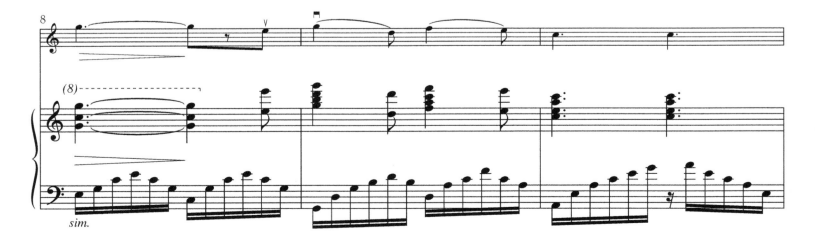

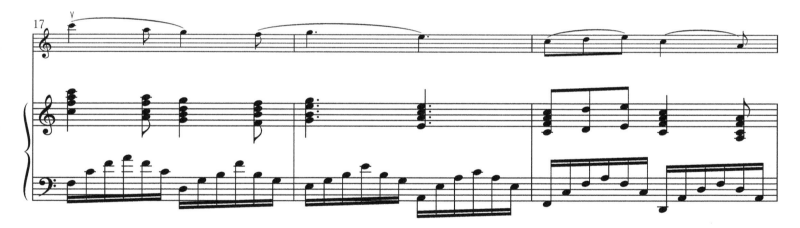

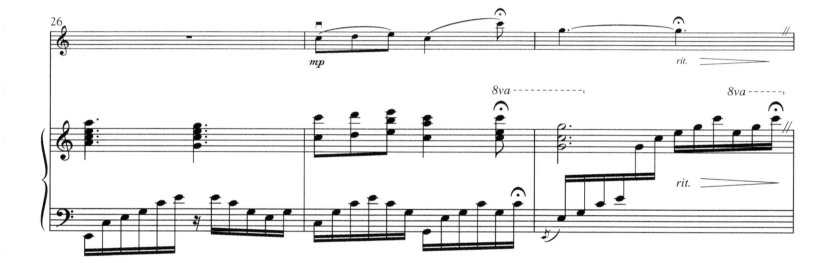

VIOLIN PART
Contents

ISBN 978-0-634-04634-6

RICORDI

DISTRIBUTED BY

HAL•LEONARD®

7777 W. BLUEMOUND RD. P.O. BOX 13819 MILWAUKEE, WI 53213

www.halleonard.com
www.ricordi.com

Quando men vo
(When I go out)

LA BOHÈME
(The Bohemian Life)

Giacomo Puccini

VIOLIN

Ch'ella mi creda
(Let her believe)

LA FANCIULLA DEL WEST
(The Girl of the Golden West)

Giacomo Puccini

VIOLIN

O mio babbino caro
(O my beloved daddy)

GIANNI SCHICCHI

Giacomo Puccini

VIOLIN

Un bel dì, vedremo
(One fine day, he will return)
MADAMA BUTTERFLY

Giacomo Puccini

VIOLIN

In quelle trine morbide
(In those soft curtains)
MANON LESCAUT

Giacomo Puccini

VIOLIN

Senza mamma
(Without a mother)

SUOR ANGELICA
(Sister Angelica)

Giacomo Puccini

VIOLIN

Recondita armonia
(Secret harmonies)
TOSCA

Giacomo Puccini

VIOLIN

Vissi d'arte
(I lived for art)
TOSCA

Giacomo Puccini

VIOLIN

E lucevan le stelle
(And the stars were shining)

TOSCA

Giacomo Puccini

VIOLIN

Nessun dorma
(None shall sleep)
TURANDOT

Giacomo Puccini

VIOLIN

Senza mamma
(Without a mother)

SUOR ANGELICA
(Sister Angelica)

Giacomo Puccini

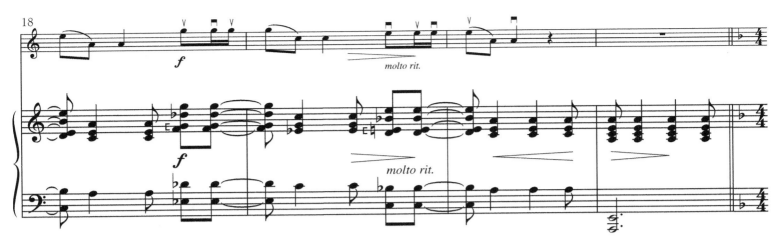

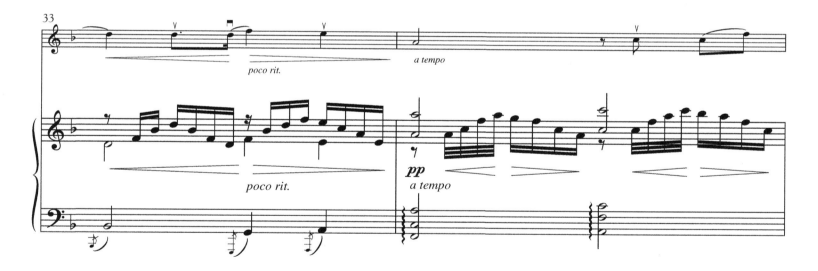

24

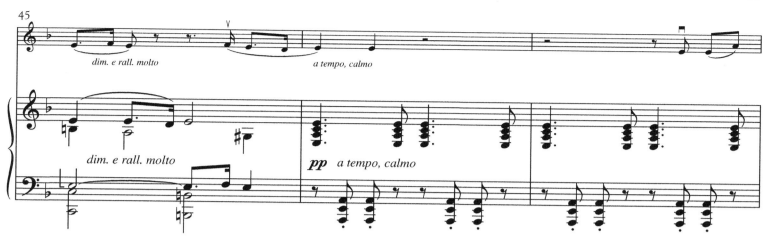

Recondita armonia
(Secret harmonies)
TOSCA

Giacomo Puccini

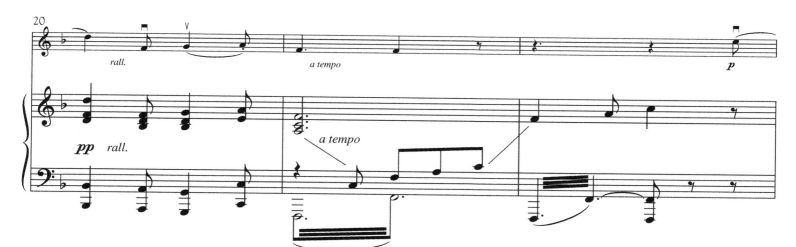

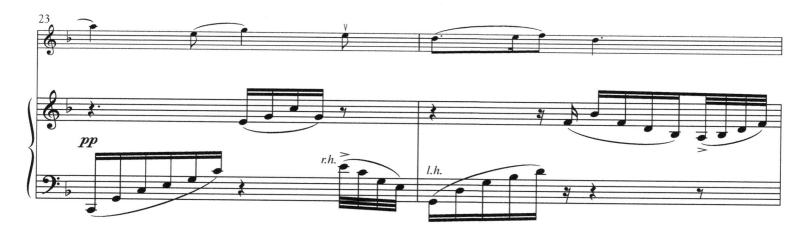

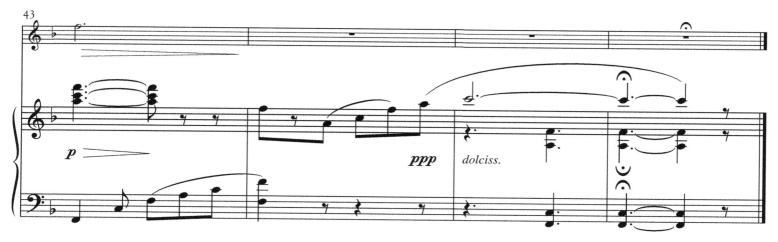

Vissi d'arte
(I lived for art)
TOSCA

Giacomo Puccini

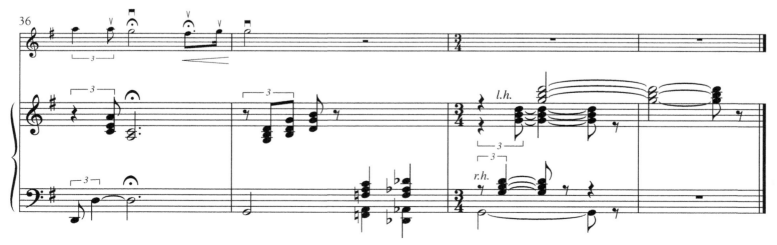

E lucevan le stelle
(And the stars were shining)
TOSCA

Giacomo Puccini

Nessun dorma
(None shall sleep)
TURANDOT

Giacomo Puccini

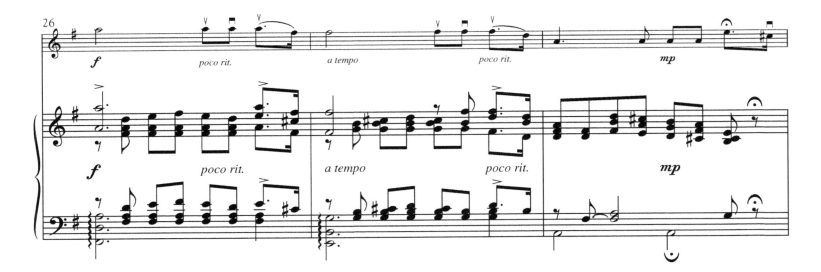

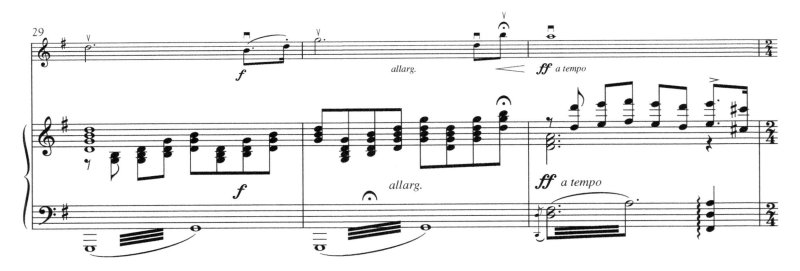